ERLII
A REFUGEE'S STORY

By: Dr. Mamadou Ibra Sy

Illustrations by: Maija Fuentes

A portion of the proceeds from the sales of this book will go to Lutheran Social Services of the National Capital Area (LSS/NCA) to support refugee children

ERLIT is a 6 year old boy with big dreams who lives with his dad, his mom, his 3 older brothers and 2 younger sisters in a small but beautiful village called IDIN.

IDIN is in the far and beautiful country of
BILDI. There, ERLIT has a beautiful house
and a lovely home. He has several pets
and has a name for each.

Every morning, ERLIT walks miles to get to school. He crosses rivers and streams. He plays along the way, chasing rabbits and squirrels. His days are long and tiring, but he always had fun!

And when he gets home from school, he plays with his brothers and sisters and shares his toys with them. He plays with his pets too. ERLIT is a happy boy!

One day, he returns from school and finds his home very quiet. His parents, brothers, and sisters are all gone. His pets fled too. His toys are scattered all over the front yard and left alone. ERLIT is all alone too. He calls the name of his parents, brothers, and sisters, but no one answers.

ERLIT runs to his friend, GONKO. There, he learns that his family has fled that morning to MAGO. MAGO is a safe place. ERLIT is sad. GONKO's dad decides to take him to MAGO to reunite with his family. They walked for 2 days through a dense and dangerous forest to get there. ERLIT is happy to see his family!

But he is also sad to learn that IDIN is
no longer home. His family tells him
that the morning he left for school, war
and its destructive power came roaring.
Peace came crumbling. Dreams were
shattered. Sadness and tears spread
like rivers. They fled.

In MAGO, ERLIT has no school. In MAGO, ERLIT has no friends. He needs to make new friends. Many of his friends in IDIN have fled to other countries. Now, they are all called REFUGEES. They have no home.

Soon, war reaches MAGO. ERLIT and his family are no longer safe. They have to flee again. But no country wants to take them. ERLIT, his parents, his brothers and sisters are scared. They can no longer sleep. ERLIT is nervous. His family will have to leave everything again!

Then comes hope! The United States of America offers to take ERLIT and his family and give them a permanent home. They are welcomed with open arms and friendly smiles. Their new neighbors give them clothes, beds, and food. They are finally safe!

ERLIT, his brothers and sisters are in school. He has a puppy that he calls IDIN. His dad and his mom are working and taking care of the family.

ERLIT has many friends. He lives in a safe
neighborhood. He plays with his friends at a local
park. At last, ERLIT and his family are no longer
refugees. They call the United States "Home".
ERLIT is happy and has big dreams!

But ERLIT never stops thinking about his friends in IDIN, including GONKO and his neighbors. He also thinks of his friends in MAGO. Are they still there? Are they safe? Do they have food? Did they flee again? Where did they go? Were they welcomed somewhere else? Will they ever see each other? Will they one day play together in the United States? ERLIT wants to welcome them, just like he was welcomed!

How can you help ERLIT and people like him?

1. Learn more about refugees

2. Tell your friends to buy the book to support refugees

3. Donate clothes, shoes, books, school supplies, etc. to refugee children

4. Find a refugee and become his/her friend

List below 4 other ways you can help ERLIT and people like him

1.

2.

3.

4.

TEST YOUR KNOWLEDGE

TRUE OR FALSE?

PEOPLE DON'T CHOOSE TO BECOME REFUGEES

Your Answer:

TRUE OR FALSE?

REFUGEES ARE PEOPLE

Your Answer:

TRUE OR FALSE?

REFUGEES ARE GOOD NEIGHBORS

Your Answer:

TRUE OR FALSE?

THE UNITED STATES IS A NATION OF REFUGEES

Your Answer:

TRUE OR FALSE?

REFUGEES STRENGTHEN OUR COUNTRY

Your Answer:

TRUE OR FALSE?

ALBERT EINSTEIN WAS A REFUGEE

Your Answer:

THE END

Made in the USA
Lexington, KY
01 August 2019